Do Fed Regulations Mortality?

Robert W. Hahn,
Randall W. Lutter,
and W. Kip Viscusi

T0273120

AEI-Brookings Joint Center for Regulatory Studies

WASHINGTON, D.C.

2000

The authors would like to thank Jonathan Wiener for excellent comments and Irene Chan and Beth Mader for helpful assistance.

To order call toll free 1-800-462-6420 or 1-717-794-3800. For all other inquiries please contact the AEI Press, 1150 Seventeenth Street, N.W., Washington, D.C. 20036 or call 1-800-862-5801.

ISBN 0-8447-7153-8

1 3 5 7 9 10 8 6 4 2

ISBN 978-1-5249-2921-3

The AEI Press
Publisher for the American Enterprise Institute
1150 17th Street, N.W.
Washington, D.C. 20036

Contents

Foreword

This volume is one in a series commissioned by the AEI-Brookings Joint Center for Regulatory Studies to contribute to the continuing debate over regulatory reform. The series will address several fundamental issues in regulation, including the design of effective reforms, the impact of proposed reforms on the public, and the political and institutional forces that affect reform.

Many forms of regulation have grown dramatically in recent decades—especially in the areas of environment, health, and safety. Moreover, expenditures in those areas are likely to continue to grow faster than the rate of government spending. Yet, the economic impact of regulation receives much less scrutiny than direct, budgeted government spending. We believe that policymakers need to rectify that imbalance.

The federal government has made substantial progress in reforming economic regulation—principally by deregulating prices and reducing entry barriers in specific industries. For example, over the past two decades consumers have realized major gains from the deregulation of transportation services. Still, policymakers can achieve significant additional gains from fully deregulating other industries, such as telecommunications and electricity.

While deregulating specific industries has led to substantial economywide gains, the steady rise in social regulation—which includes not only environmental, health, and safety standards but many other government-imposed rights and benefits—has had mixed results. Entrepreneurs increasingly face an assortment of employer mandates and legal liabilities that dictate decisions about products, payrolls, and personnel practices. Several scholars have questioned the wisdom of that expansion in social regulation. Some regulations, such as the phaseout of lead in gasoline, have been quite successful, while others, such as the requirement for safety caps on aspirin bottles, have led to increased risks. As those regulatory activities grow, so does the need to consider their implications more carefully.

We do not take the view that all regulation is bad or that all proposed reforms are good. We should judge regulations by their individual benefits and costs, which in the past have varied widely. Similarly, we should judge reform proposals on the basis of their likely benefits and costs. The important point is that, in an era when regulation appears to impose very substantial costs in the form of higher consumer prices and lower economic output, carefully weighing the likely benefits and costs of rules and reform proposals is essential for defining an appropriate scope for regulatory activity.

The debates over regulatory policy have often been highly partisan and ill-informed. We hope that this series will help illuminate many of the complex issues involved in designing and implementing regulation and regulatory reforms at all levels of government.

ROBERT W. HAHN
ROBERT E. LITAN
AEI-Brookings Joint Center
for Regulatory Studies

Executive Summary

A minimal test of the desirability of regulations is that they further their primary objectives. In some cases, regulations designed to reduce health, safety, and environmental risks can actually increase risk, especially when such regulations lead to significant reductions in private expenditures on life-saving investments. This monograph assesses the mortality implications of the costs of a group of twenty-four federal health, safety, and environmental regulations.

We find that an unintended increase in risk is likely to result from the majority of regulations examined here. A more positive result is that aggregate mortality risk falls for the entire set of regulations, primarily because a few regulations yield large reductions in risk.

We believe that such analysis can help to highlight the potential problems with inefficient regulation and can serve as a useful complement to other forms of analysis, such as benefit-cost analysis. Specifically, we believe that an assessment of the mortality implications of regulatory costs can and should be used to help identify those regulations whose primary purpose is to save lives but that may have the unintended consequence of actually increasing mortality. In such perverse cases, Congress and the regulatory agencies should seriously consider alternatives that would yield higher levels of economic welfare and save more lives.

1

Introduction

The costs of federal environmental, health, and safety regulation have grown dramatically in recent decades and are now on the order of $200 billion annually.[1] Those costs appear likely to increase significantly over the next decade as well, because of legislative and regulatory mandates that are not yet met.

Much environmental, health, and safety regulation has been criticized because it either does not pass a benefit-cost test or because it could be much more effective in achieving specified objectives.[2] For example, regulations aimed at saving or extending lives differ dramatically in terms of their cost-effectiveness.[3] Indeed, ample research suggests that policymakers could significantly improve regulation so as to save more lives with fewer resources.[4] One study found that a reallocation of mandated expenditures toward those regulations with the highest payoff to society could save as many as 60,000 more lives per year at no additional cost.[5]

Another concern arises when regulations intended to reduce risk in fact increase it.[6] The notion that regulations designed to reduce environmental, health, and safety risks can actually increase them is not new.[7] Viscusi, for example, identifies three reasons regulations can increase risk.[8]

First, a regulation can lead to behavioral responses that offset the intended impact of the regulation. For example, drivers required to wear seat belts may be more inclined to drive faster and would thereby offset the reduced risk to the drivers and increase risks to pedestrians and other drivers.

Second, the act of complying with regulations may pose risks. For example, removing asbestos from schools can increase exposure; earthmoving equipment used to clean up hazardous waste sites increases workers' risks of fatalities and injuries; and substitutes to pesticides and harmful consumer products often pose some risk.[9]

Third, the costs of compliance with regulations pose risks. Compliance typically reduces the amount of private resources that people have to spend on a wide range of activities, including health care, children's education, and automobile safety. When people have fewer resources, they spend less to reduce risks. The resulting increase in risk offsets the direct reduction in risk attributable to a government action. Moreover, if that direct risk reduction is small and the regulation is *very* ineffective relative to its cost, then total risk could rise instead of fall.

Those three unintended consequences may exist for any environmental, health, or safety regulation that reduces private expenditures on life-saving investments. We focus here on the third effect—the risk implications of regulatory costs—because it has the broadest potential applicability.

The novel aspect of this monograph is our assessment of the mortality implications of regulatory costs of a large group of federal regulations. We investigate whether those regulations are likely to have the unintended effect of increasing the mortality risk they seek to reduce. We find that an unintended increase in total risk is likely to occur for the majority of regulations examined here. At the same time, aggregate mortality risk falls for those regulations, in large part because a few regulations yield large reductions in risk. Such analysis can highlight the potential problems with regulation and can be a useful complement to other forms of analysis, such as benefit-cost analysis.

Section 2 reviews important themes in the literature linking income and health and evaluates that methodological approach. In section 3, we present a group of economically significant federal regulations whose primary benefit is to reduce mortality. We then project how mortality estimates for those regulations are likely to change when one takes into account the effects of income on private risk reduction. Section 4 discusses some implications of our work and suggests areas for further research.

2
Wealthier Is Healthier

Researchers have most extensively analyzed the effect of income on health and safety for the case of mortality risk. Dozens of articles in economics and public health journals substantiate the claim that richer people live longer.[10] Simple correlations of annual death rates and income suggest that a community whose income rises by about $10 million can expect about one fewer death.[11]

There is little debate about the existence of a relationship between income and mortality. An important part of health is related to spending resources on reducing risks—for example, going to the doctor when one is sick. To the extent that we allocate more resources to ill-conceived regulations that do little to reduce risk, we remove private resources from risk-reducing activities and thereby raise mortality risk.

In the U.S. regulatory arena, the argument that regulations whose cost-effectiveness exceeds an identifiable limit would raise rather than lower risk has a rich history. Wildavsky first articulated the idea in 1980, and Keeney first formalized it.[12] The idea was introduced in regulatory debates pertaining to air quality in the 1980s.[13] In 1991 an opinion by the U.S. Court of Appeals for the D.C. Circuit concerning a worker safety standard issued by the Occupational Safety and Health Administration cited Keeney's seminal article.[14] Later, the head of the regulatory affairs office at the Office of Management and Budget wrote to OSHA asking it to investigate that effect in the context of a different standard. The resulting controversy led to congressional hearings, various articles in major newspapers, and considerable academic interest.[15]

Viscusi edited a special issue of the *Journal of Risk and Uncertainty* that was dedicated to the topic.[16] Cross provided an overview of the role of analysis identifying mortality consequences of regulatory expenditures.[17] Sunstein argued that courts should find that regulations that raise risks rather than lower them are arbitrary and capricious.[18] Graham and Wiener described risk-risk tradeoffs generally and showed their importance for a wide variety of regulatory issues.[19]

This monograph relies on recent work by Lutter, Morrall, and Viscusi, because it provides a theoretical basis for estimating the linkage between mortality and income. Those authors estimated that an increase in income of about $15 million in a large U.S. population reduces mortality risk by one statistical death.[20] To estimate that relationship they construct a model in which people can reduce their risk of death through self-protective measures, but risk increases with increases in risky behaviors, such as smoking, overdrinking, and being overweight. McGinnis and Foege estimated that those three risky behaviors account for 38 percent of all deaths in the United States.[21] Lutter, Morrall, and Viscusi used cross-sectional data to estimate the elasticities of those behaviors with respect to income. Incorporating those elasticities into their model, they calculated that the decline in income associated with one additional induced fatality is about $15 million. Of course, other cutoffs may be appropriate for other populations. For example, Pritchett and Summers estimated a relationship between infant mortality in developing countries that can be used to calculate the additional income level needed to avoid a statistical death. An income gain of about $.3 million in India would on average avert one infant death.[22]

Lutter, Morrall, and Viscusi use causal mechanisms linking those risky behaviors to risk of death to explain most of the simple association between income and mortality observed in earlier work. Without such causal mechanisms, it was unclear whether the association reflected a causal relationship from income to health or from health to income. After all, sick people are more likely to lose their jobs and have lower incomes. It was also unclear whether an omitted third variable confounded the association. For example, people endowed with patience or perseverance may save financial capital, invest in human capital, and preserve their own health more than others. In that case there would be a noncausal association between health and income that researchers might erroneously interpret as causal. Lutter, Morrall, and Viscusi showed that risky behaviors rise with lower incomes and that the mortality implications of those risky behaviors explain most of the previously reported correlations between income and mortality. Their results improve our confidence that estimates of the effect of income on mortality reflect a causal relationship.

Ettner provided new evidence on the relationship between income and a number of other health measures.[23] She reported that increases in income have a large beneficial effect on mental and physical health. She used three different data sets with samples ranging from 8,000 to 30,000 people. The data sets included information on mental and physical health using self-assessed health status, work limitations, bed days, average daily consumption of alcohol, and scales of depressive symptoms and alcoholic behavior. Most important, Ettner found that the estimated effects of income on health changed little when she used statistical methods to ensure that her estimates reflected only the net causal effect of income on health. She recommended that benefit-cost analyses of government programs that may reduce disposable income take into account potential adverse effects on morbidity.

Smith recently offered several interpretations of the observed relationship between income and health.[24] We consider those here because they help to highlight the strengths and limitations of the approach taken by mainstream economists. The first interpretation states that lower income is associated with higher mortality because of the cumulative toll of small stresses and episodic wear and tear on bodily systems, which is presumed to be higher among lower-income people. That interpretation is consistent with the analysis by Lutter, Morrall, and Viscusi. It says that a causal relationship from income to health exists, but that it takes some time to be fully manifested. It implies that stress-related changes, not income per se, are the relevant cause. If income changes are used as an index of stress, however, then that interpretation is consistent.

A second interpretation of the association between income and health is driven by deprivation in early childhood, which causes physiological problems manifested much later in adult life. Under that interpretation, the observed relationship results because low parental income implies a poor home environment during pregnancy or early infancy. Thus, a poor environment early in life causes poor health in middle age or later. The causal link from regulatory costs to poor health is thus intergenerational and may occur with a lag of fifty years or more. That interpretation is not compatible with the analysis by Lutter, Morrall, and Viscusi. It suggests a more indirect linkage between income and mortality and would require a different set of data and models to test. Recent evidence suggests that the importance of that interpretation is limited. Lamont et al. report that "adult lifestyle and biological risk markers were the most important determinants of cardiovascular health . . . at age 49–51."[25] Although socioeconomic position at birth and birth weight were negatively associated with measures of the risk of cardiovascular disease, only social class at birth in women was statistically significant. Moreover, early life variables accounted for only 2.2 percent and 2.0 percent of the total variance in men and women, respectively. Those effects are far less than the 3.4 percent and 7.6 percent of variance explained by adult socioeconomic position and lifestyle.[26]

A third interpretation is that low *relative* income increases psychosocial stress, which worsens health by adversely affecting endocrine and immunological processes. That interpretation is not compatible with the Lutter, Morrall, and Viscusi thesis—although both could be valid—because it implies that socioeconomic status is what matters, not absolute levels of income. In that case a regulation that lowered the income of all families by a given percentage without affecting the distribution would not necessarily worsen health.

But a measurement problem plagues the work purporting to show a relationship between inequality and mortality. Given that mortality risk falls at a decreasing rate as incomes rise, community studies of income inequality and mortality will generally show an association between income inequality and mortality, even when inequality has no causal effect on mortality. As an example, consider two families with median income that have different fortunes—so the income of one falls by 10 percent while the income of the other rises by 10 percent. With a nonlinear causal relationship between income and mortality, mortality would rise because the mortality increase for the family whose income fell would be greater than the mortality decrease for the family whose income rose. Attributing the increase in mortality to the increase in income inequality is unwarranted because it could instead be due simply to the diminishing effect of higher income on health. Without accounting for that effect, it is therefore premature to conclude that relative income has a causal effect on mortality risk. Of course, the thesis is not necessarily wrong; declines in relative income may in fact worsen psychosocial stress and increase mortality risks. But we discount that interpretation, given the lack of credible empirical support.

The preceding review suggests that some reasonably strong evidence supports a causal linkage between income and mortality.

3

Mortality Implications of the Costs of Recent Federal Regulations

In this study we retain the interpretation of the income-mortality relationship as Lutter, Morrall, and Viscusi estimated it. In particular, we assume that a decline in income of $15 million, if shared among a large population, leads to an increase in expected mortality of one. We go beyond Lutter, Morrall, and Viscusi by assessing the mortality implications of their research for a nearly complete set of recent federal regulations, whose primary effect is to reduce mortality risk.

Before turning to the results of our analysis, we note several key assumptions. First, regarding the income-mortality relationship, we follow Lutter, Morrall, and Viscusi and assume that the income elasticities estimated in the equations for the demand to engage in risky behaviors measure causal relationships and are not significantly confounded by missing variables such as perseverance or patience. We also assume that the increase in mortality predicted to occur with a decline in income occurs more or less at the same time that income declines. But to the extent that income changes affect risky behaviors that in turn influence mortality risk only after several years, the length of the period during which mortality risks change may be quite long. For example, Lutter, Morrall, and Viscusi assumed that the incremental increases in mortality occured during a period extending from age thirty-eight to age seventy-eight, the age when half of thirty-five-year-olds have died. Thus, it is possible that the mortality increases associated with changes in income are manifested years after the changes in income initially occur. The cross-sectional analyses of Keeney and others are silent on the timing of income-related changes in mortality risk. A delay between income changes and mortality changes that is not reflected in the Lutter, Morrall, and Viscusi analysis would increase the income loss associated with an additional induced fatality. We address that issue in our sensitivity analysis by considering an income cutoff of $50 million.[27]

Second, with respect to regulations for which we are estimating induced increases in mortality, we assume that costs are distributed neutrally among different income groups, an assumption consistent with the approach of Lutter, Morrall, and Viscusi, who developed estimates appropriate for a representative consumer. That assumption is important because the effect of income on mortality is greater among low-income groups than among high-income groups.[28] Thus, if costs were borne disproportionately among the rich, then the induced increases in mortality risk would be lower than our estimate. On the other hand, if costs in fact fall disproportionately on the poor, then our estimates of induced increases in mortality risk are conservative.[29]

To substantiate our assumption, we first note that the accepted view is that the costs of most environmental programs are distributed somewhat regressively.[30] In addition, we reexamined the agencies' economic analysis of each rule to see whether it discussed the distribution of costs directly or indirectly. We found no good discussion of how costs would be distributed by income level. We conclude there-fore that our assumption is consistent with available data and unlikely to bias upward our estimates of induced mor-tality.

Third, we assume that the rules do not lead to significant transfers. Transfers have induced mortality effects to the extent that the effect of income on mortality is greater among the poor than the rich. To check that such an assumption is warranted, we reexamined the regulatory impact analyses for the set of rules described above with an eye toward discovering significant transfers either among private parties or between the government and private par-ties. For the set of rules we examined, the regulatory impact analyses had no discussion of significant transfers. From our reading of the rules, we found no evidence that such trans-fers were likely.[31] Thus, we use the agency's estimates of the aggregate social cost as a measure of the income change induced by the regulation. For rules with offsetting cost sav-ings, such as those related to reduced fire damage, we net such cost savings from social cost estimates before calculat-ing induced mortality.

We address the uncertainty in the estimated effect of income on mortality by using a range of values for the income-mortality cutoff from $10 million to $50 million.[32] We use the $15 million estimate of Lutter, Morrall, and Viscusi as a best estimate.

We begin with a database of essentially all final regula-tions issued by federal agencies to reduce environmental, health, or safety risks between 1991 and June 1998. Hahn previously compiled a database that included all regulations issued between 1991 and the middle of 1996 and classified as major or economically significant under the two execu-tive orders addressing regulatory review, Executive Order 12291 and Executive Order 12866.[33] To that set we added rules from the middle of 1996 until 1998 that were analyzed as part of the AEI-Brookings Joint Center Regulatory Improvement Project.[34]

We limit our analysis to those regulations that we estimate had mortality benefits that were at least 90 percent of total benefits, according to agency estimates.[35] Those regulations are the most logical candidates for our analysis because their primary effect is to reduce mortality risk. A regulation to promote fair lending, for example, even if it did not pass a benefit-cost test, might be assessed in terms of its net effect on fair lending, but not its effect on mortality risk, which seems unrelated and irrelevant. On the other hand, an analytic finding that a regulation designed to reduce mortality risk instead increased it would seem to be of substantial policy interest.[36]

A key difficulty in assessing summary measures of the benefits and costs of federal regulations is the treatment of uncertainty. Some economic analyses present point estimates of costs or benefits, while others use ranges.[37] For simplicity we convert ranges to point estimates by taking their midpoint unless the agency has indicated a best estimate. That simplification may introduce an unknown bias in our results to the extent that the underlying distributions of benefits or costs are systematically skewed toward the upper or lower bounds of the range.

Key summary statistics for the twenty-four regulations in our data set appear in table 3-1.[38] We define the variables presented in the table as follows. Gross cost is the social cost estimated by the agency. For rules Hahn analyzed in his 1996 study, we follow his methods. For rules issued after 1996 and excluded from Hahn's study, we replicate the Hahn procedure by calculating annualized cost using a 5 percent discount rate, the agency's estimates of the nonrecurring capital cost and the operation and maintenance cost, and the agency's period of annualization. Net cost is gross

Table 3-1 Costs, Benefits, and Cost per Statistical Life of Individual Regulations at an Income-Mortality Cutoff of $15 Million

Rule	Agency	Year
Toxicity characteristics to determine hazardous wastes	EPA	1990
Underground storage tanks: technical requirements	EPA	1988
Manufactured home construction and safety standards on wind standards	HUD	1994
Process safety management of highly hazardous chemicals	DOL	1992
Regulations restricting the sale and distribution of cigarettes and smokeless tobacco to protect children and adolescents	HHS	1996
Medicare and Medicaid programs: hospital conditions of participation; identification of potential organ, tissue, and eye donors; and transplant hospitals' provision of transplant-related data	HHS	1998
Quality mammography standards	HHS	1997
Food labeling regulations	HHS	1993
Childproof lighters	CPSC	1993
Standard for occupational exposure to benzene	DOL	1987
Occupational exposure to methylene chloride	DOL	1997
Occupational exposure to 4,4' methylenedianiline	DOL	1992
Asbestos: manufacture, importation, processing, and distribution in commerce—prohibitions (total)	EPA	1989
National primary and secondary water regulations—phase II: maximum contaminant levels for 38 contaminants	EPA	1991
Occupational exposure to asbestos	DOL	1994
Hazardous waste management system—wood preservatives	EPA	1990
Sewage sludge use and disposal regulations, 40 CFR pt. 503	EPA	1993
Land disposal restrictions for "third third" scheduled wastes	EPA	1990
Hazardous waste management system: final solvents and dioxins land disposal restrictions rule	EPA	1986
Occupational exposure to formaldehyde	DOL	1987
Prohibit the land disposal of the first third of scheduled wastes ("second sixth" proposal)	EPA	1988
Land disposal restrictions—phase II: universal treatment standards and treatment standards for organic toxicity, characteristic wastes, and newly listed wastes	EPA	1994
Drinking water regulations, synthetic organic chemicals—phase V	EPA	1992
Solid waste disposal facility criteria, 40 CFR pt. 257 and pt. 258	EPA	1991
Total		

Notes: All values are millions of 1995 dollars annually; the income-mortality cutoff of $15 million (1990 dollars) has been converted to $17.3 million. Rules are ranked in order of decreasing cost-effectiveness.

Estimates of induced mortality changes resulting from regulatory costs are based on net costs, that is, costs less cost savings. Negative fatalities induced by a rule indicate statistical lives saved.

Agencies include the Environmental Protection Agency (EPA), the Department of Housing and Urban Development (HUD), the Department of Labor (DOL), the Department of Health and Human Services (HHS), and the Consumer Product Safety Commission (CPSC).

Gross Cost	Cost Savings	Net Costs	Monetized Benefits	Discounted Statistical Lives Saved	Net Cost per Discounted Statistical Life	Fatalities Induced by Cost of Rules	Net Lives Saved by Rules
230	630	−400	.17	.048	−8,300	−23	23
3,300	3,700	−390	3.9	1.1	−350	−22	24
56	110	−55	8 1	1.5	−37	−3.2	4.7
650	1,400	−720	1,200	220	−3.3	−42	260
170	2,500	−2,400	56,000	4,700	−.50	−140	4,900
160	0	160	3,800	710	.22	9.2	700
40	16	24	140	75	.32	1.4	74
160	0	180	2,000	520	.35	10	510
92	42	50	520	95	.53	2.9	92
32	0	32	16	4.4	7.1	1.8	2.6
100	0	100	130	12	8.5	5.9	6.2
12	0	12	2.5	.70	18	.71	−.010
74	0	74	14	3.9	19	4.3	−.41
1,100	0	1,100	160	44	25	63	−19
340	0	340	49	13	27	20	−7.1
14	0	14	1.0	.29	50	.83	−.55
45	0	45	.86	.24	190	2.6	−2.3
520	1.2	510	10	2.8	190	30	−27
200	0	200	3.6	1.0	200	12	−11
82	0	82	.75	.21	390	4.8	−4.5
1,100	0	1,100	10	2.9	400	66	−63
220	79	140	.56	.16	910	8.3	−8.2
59	0	59	.022	.0061	9,600	3.4	−3.4
190	9.2	180	.017	.0049	36,000	10	−10
9,000	**8,500**	**520**	**64,000**	**6,400**	**.081**	**30**	**6,400**

cost less cost savings, where cost savings are offsetting benefits or reductions in cost identified by the agencies. Examples of major cost savings include reduced wind damage to third parties, reduced groundwater cleanup costs, and reduced fire damage. Although other analysts might treat those cost savings as benefits, we prefer to treat them as cost savings because they serve to increase the income of households and therefore affect the measure of cost that we wish to use in assessing how income changes may affect mortality risk.[39]

Following Hahn's 1996 methodology, we calculate health benefits to identify rules for which mortality-related benefits are at least 90 percent of total benefits. We make adjustments to agency estimates when they depart from what we believe to be best practice.[40] First, we convert premature fatalities averted to life-years gained, by multiplying the statistical lives saved by an estimate of the life-years gained per premature death averted that is specific for a given cause of death and derived from estimates in the literature.[41] Second, we discount for latency by using periods that vary by cause of death and are based on estimates in the literature.[42] That gives us discounted statistical life-years saved.[43]

Monetized benefits, the seventh column in table 3-1, include the value of the years of life gained, calculated at $313,000 per life-year, and any other benefits presented by the agency.[44] We calculate discounted change in mortality risk, presented in the next column, by using agency estimates of the change in population mortality risk, the latency period, the discount factor, and the annualization period discussed above. The net cost per statistical life saved is the net cost divided by the discounted reduction in population mortality risk.

In estimating induced fatalities, we follow two alternative approaches to deal with categories of benefits other than mortality. First, we simply ignore them because they are small, that is, less than 10 percent of total benefits. Second, we assume that they have exactly the same effects on mortality as an increase in income and so subtract them from the costs. Our results are essentially the same for both approaches. In table 3-1 we present the results from our first approach.

The cost-effectiveness of the rules listed in the table varies tremendously. We order the rules by increasing cost—net of cost savings—per statistical life saved.[45] For five regulations the cost is negative because of large cost savings. For four others the cost is positive but substantially less than $1 million per statistical life saved. For two others the cost is billions of dollars per statistical life saved. Risk reduction for rules with similar cost can vary by as much as a factor of 100,000. Thus, substantial opportunities appear to exist to increase the number of lives saved for a given expenditure of resources.[46]

The ordering of the rules in table 3-1 permits a simple identification of those rules that pass a benefit-cost test. The first nine rules in the table pass because they have a net cost per statistical life saved of less than $5 million. The other fifteen rules fail.

To calculate the induced fatalities, we divide the net costs presented in the table by the income-mortality cutoff estimated by Lutter, Morrall, and Viscusi—$15 million dollars per statistical life saved.[47] The result is the change in mortality attributable to the changes in income that result from the rule. The final column in the table, net statistical lives saved by the rule, is the estimate of net reductions in mortality—the mortality risk reduction directly attributable to the rule less the mortality risk increases associated with reduced income.

The majority of rules actually raise mortality risk on net at an income-mortality cutoff of $15 million, as figure 3-1

Figure 3-1 Effects of Regulations on Mortality

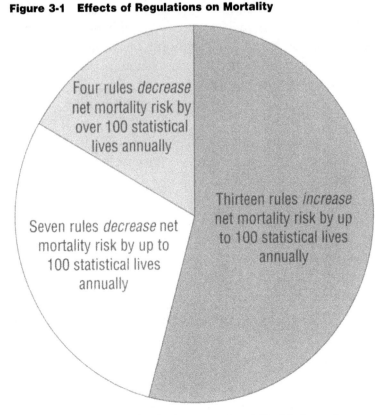

Note: Among the thirteen rules that increase net mortality risk, the maximum number of fatalities induced by a rule is sixty-six.

shows. At that cutoff, the total increase in mortality—among rules that increased mortality—was 230 expected deaths, although the reductions in mortality from a handful of rules swamped that. The total net reduction in mortality from all rules is 6,400. Thus, the full impact on mortality risk for all twenty-four regulations was beneficial.

Since uncertainty exists about whether an income loss of $15 million in a large population indeed causes one additional fatality, we also use a more conservative approach. In that approach we use a cutoff of $50 million, proposed by Viscusi,[48] and find that eight rules fail. We also use a cutoff

Figure 3-2 Rules Failing an Income-Mortality or Benefit-Cost Test

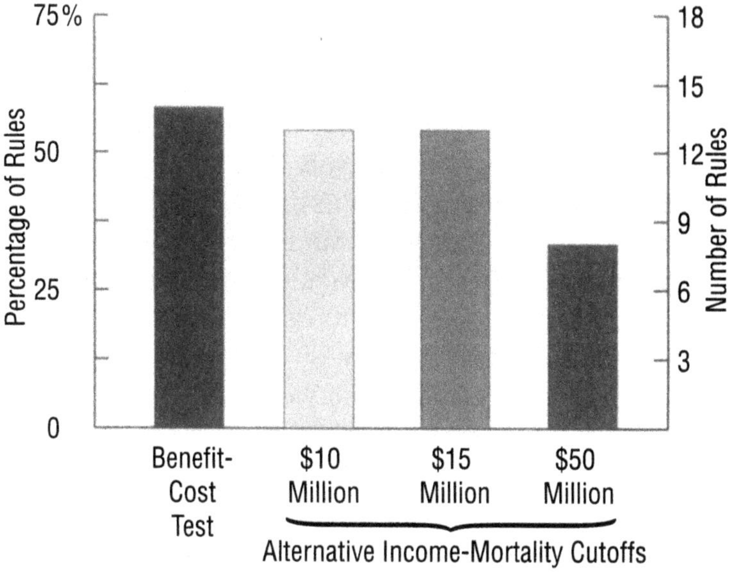

Note: Twenty-four rules were analyzed.

of $10 million and find that thirteen of the twenty-four rules increase mortality. See figure 3-2. Thus, the net mortality effects appear to be somewhat sensitive to the cutoff value we assume for our calculations. We also note that with a cutoff of $50 million instead of $15 million, the total net change in mortality declines by only twenty statistical lives.

To test the sensitivity of our analysis to other variables, we also varied the discount rate and latency periods used in our calculations. While in the base case the number of rules that failed the income-mortality test was thirteen, that number fell to ten with a discount rate of 3 percent. Thirteen rules failed at a discount rate of 7 percent. Assuming no latency—that is, no delay between exposure and onset of health effects—nine rules fail.

Rules with large numbers of induced fatalities exhibit two patterns. First, they are disproportionately the Environmental

Protection Agency's rules. In terms of their net effect on mortality, the EPA issued six of the worst eight and only two of the best eight. By contrast, the Department of Health and Human Services did not issue any rules that fell among the worst eight and issued four of the best eight rules. Second, the six EPA rules that raise mortality risks are all intended to reduce exposure to carcinogens in the environment.

Other researchers have found similar patterns. Tengs et al. reported that government interventions to reduce exposure to toxic chemicals in the environment are the least cost-effective of the interventions that they considered. They also reported that the EPA's regulations were least cost-effective of the categories that they identified.[49] In addition, Hahn reported that federal regulations limiting exposure to carcinogens are less cost-effective than other regulations and that EPA regulations reducing exposure to carcinogens are less cost-effective still.[50]

Although estimates of induced mortality are uncertain, so, too, are the benefits of environmental, health, and safety regulations. Therefore, we can best examine the implications of the uncertainty of estimates of induced mortality in a risk assessment that takes into account all sources of uncertainty.

4

Conclusions

In this monograph we assess how the adverse health implications of regulatory costs affect mortality risk by considering a broad group of federal regulations. We find that an unintended increase in risk is likely to occur for over half the regulations examined here. Even with conservative assumptions, an unintended increase would occur in a third of the rules in our database. But no basis exists for the claim that government regulations in general are so costly as to raise mortality risk. Indeed, aggregate mortality risk falls for the regulations examined here, in large part because a few regulations yield large reductions in risk, particularly regulations on teens' tobacco use, donated organs, and food labeling.

While we are comfortable with the broad conclusions that flow from this analysis, we believe that more research is needed to determine the precise relationship between income and health and its implications for regulatory policy. In particular, researchers could investigate how that relationship varies with age, income level, and the extent of delays between income changes and resulting changes in health risks. Researchers could also assess the implications of income changes on longevity. Finally, the relationship between income and morbidity and injuries also merits further study.

We have witnessed a great deal of debate about the validity and merit of estimates of the mortality implications of regulatory costs. Our analysis can help to highlight potential problems with regulation and can serve as a useful complement to other forms of analysis, such as benefit-cost analysis. Specifically, we believe that assessments of the mortality implications of regulatory costs can and should be used to help identify those regulations intended primarily to reduce mortality risks that have the unintended consequence of actually raising such risks. In such perverse cases, Congress and the regulatory agencies should seriously consider alternatives that would yield higher levels of economic welfare and help reduce the risk of death.

Appendix

In table A-1 we list the twenty-four rules we have analyzed with their *Federal Register* citations and their dates of enactment.

Table A-1
Rules and *Federal Register* Citations

Rule	Agency	Citation	Date
Childproof lighters	CPSC	58 FR 37,557	1993
Occupational exposure to 4,4' methylenedianiline	DOL	57 FR 35,630	1992
Occupational exposure to asbestos	DOL	59 FR 40,964	1994
Occupational exposure to formaldehyde	DOL	52 FR 46,168	1987
Occupational exposure to methylene chloride	DOL	62 FR 1,493	1997
Process safety management of highly hazardous chemicals	DOL	57 FR 6,403	1992
Standard for occupational exposure to benzene	DOL	52 FR 34,460	1987
Asbestos; manufacture, importation, processing, and distribution in commerce prohibitions (total)	EPA	54 FR 29,460	1989
Drinking water regulations, synthetic organic chemicals—phase V	EPA	57 FR 31,776	1992
Hazardous waste management system: final solvents and dioxins land disposal restrictions rule	EPA	51 FR 40,572	1986
Hazardous waste management system—wood preservatives	EPA	55 FR 50,450	1990
Land disposal restrictions for "third third" scheduled wastes	EPA	55 FR 22,520	1990
Land disposal restrictions—phase II: universal treatment standards and treatment standards for organic toxicity, characteristic wastes, and newly listed wastes	EPA	59 FR 47,982	1994
National primary and secondary water regulations—phase II: maximum contaminant levels for 38 contaminants	EPA	56 FR 3,526, 56 FR 30,266	1991
Prohibit the land disposal of the first third of scheduled wastes ("second sixth" proposal)	EPA	53 FR 31,138	1988
Sewage sludge use and disposal regulations	EPA	58 FR 9,248	1993
Solid waste disposal facility criteria	EPA	56 FR 50,978	1991
Toxicity characteristics to determine hazardous wastes	EPA	55 FR 11,798	1990
Underground storage tanks: technical requirements	EPA	53 FR 37,082	1988
Food labeling regulations	HHS	58 FR 2,478 (rule), 58 FR 2,927 (impact)	1993
Medicare and Medicaid programs: hospital conditions of participation; identification of potential organ, tissue, and eye donors; and transplant hospitals' provision of transplant-related data	HHS	63 FR 33,856	1998
Quality mammography standards	HHS	62 FR 55,852	1997
Regulations restricting the sale and distribution of cigarettes and smokeless tobacco to protect children and adolescents	HHS	61 FR 44,396	1996
Manufactured home construction and safety standards on wind standards	HUD	59 FR 2,456	1994

Note: Rules are listed in alphabetical order by agency and then by rule name. Agencies include the Consumer Product Safety Commission (CPSC), the Department of Labor (DOL), the Environmental Protection Agency (EPA), the Department of Health and Human Services (HHS), and the Department of Housing and Urban Development (HUD).

Notes

1. See U.S. Office of Management and Budget (1999).
2. See Hahn (1996) and Warren and Marchant (1993).
3. See Morrall (1986).
4. See Morrall (1986) and Viscusi (1996).
5. See Tengs and Graham (1996).
6. We prefer the phrase *reducing mortality risk* to the more common phrase *saving lives,* because it is more accurate. These regulatory actions lower or raise the mortality risk faced by large numbers of people only slightly. In that sense, they are fundamentally different from an effort to save a life by rescuing an identifiable victim from, say, a burning building.
7. See, for example, Wildavsky (1980) and Lave (1981).
8. See Viscusi (1994b).
9. See Viscusi and Zeckhauser (1994) and Graham and Wiener (1995).
10. See, for example, Duleep (1986) and Wolfson et al. (1992).
11. See Lutter and Morrall (1994).
12. See Keeney (1990).
13. See, for example, Steger (1988). See also the consideration of a $7.5 million income-risk cutoff in the Food and Drug Administration's 1993 food labeling regulations (U.S. Food and Drug Administration 1993).
14. See Keeney (1990).
15. See Lutter, Morrall, and Viscusi (1999) for a discussion.
16. See Viscusi (1994b).
17. See Cross (1995). Cross, following Lutter and Morrall (1994), uses the term *health–health analysis* to describe the assessment of the adverse health consequences of regulatory costs.
18. See Sunstein (1996).
19. See Graham and Wiener (1995) and Wiener (1998).

20. See Lutter, Morrall, and Viscusi (1999). These numbers are broadly consistent with analyses by Chapman and Hariharan (1994) and Keeney (1997).
21. These three behaviors account for 76 percent of all deaths with identifiable causes. See McGinnis and Foege (1993).
22. See Pritchett and Summers (1996). We derive the $300,000 estimate by applying the midpoint of the elasticities estimated by Pritchett and Summers (−.2 to −.4) to data on income and mortality for India. See Central Intelligence Agency (1998). The CIA *World Factbook* gives a purchasing-power parity GDP for 1997 of $1.5 trillion dollars and a GDP growth rate of 5 percent. When we apply that growth rate, the calculated GDP for 1998 is $1.6 trillion. The 1998 population was 980,000,000; the infant mortality rate in 1998 was sixty-three deaths per 1,000 live births; and the 1998 birth rate was twenty-six births per 1,000 population.
23. See Ettner (1996).
24. See Smith (1999).
25. See Lamont et al. (2000, 273).
26. Ibid.
27. In our analysis we convert the $50 million in 1990 dollars to $58 million in 1995 dollars.
28. See Keeney (1997) and Chapman and Hariharan (1994).
29. See Keeney (1994).
30. See, for example, Harrison (1975), Tietenberg (1996), and Walls and Hanson (1999). Cross (1995, 764) surveys the available literature and concludes that "the costs of typical environmental regulations are concentrated among the poor."
31. We exclude a regulation issued by the National Highway Traffic Safety Administration for the operation of motor vehicles by intoxicated persons that would have offered grants to states, because such grants are transfers that are not necessarily equivalent to social cost.
32. See Viscusi (1994a) for the $50 million estimate.
33. See Hahn (1999). The full set includes 115 rules promulgated by the Environmental Protection Agency, 28 by the Department of Labor, 13 by the Department of Transportation, 5 by the Department of Health and Human Services, 4 by the Department of Agriculture, 2 by the Department of Housing and Urban Development, and 1 by the Consumer Product Safety Commission. Those rules comprise virtually all major rules and a few potentially major rules. The set excludes two regulations to protect strato-

spheric ozone that have very large net benefits according to the EPA.

34. Information on the Joint Center Regulatory Improvement Project can be found at www.aei.brookings.org.

35. We use a database of twenty-four rules. Of those rules, one is from the Consumer Product Safety Commission, four from the Department of Health and Human Services, one from the Department of Housing and Urban Development, six from the Department of Labor, and twelve from the Environmental Protection Agency. We may be excluding some rules that reduce mortality but for which regulatory agencies were unable to develop quantitative estimates of benefits.

36. Some interesting theoretical issues arise in implementing the income-mortality calculation when the benefits include effects unrelated to reductions in mortality risk. Although a complete treatment of that issue is beyond the scope of our analysis, one would generally like to measure the impact of the regulation on a person's disposable income and then implement the income-mortality calculation. It is not always simple to estimate that impact when a regulation has multiple effects. In some cases, however, one can bound the calculation by using plausible assumptions about the nature of the cost and benefit functions.

37. See Hahn et al. (2000).

38. See the appendix for a list of the twenty-four regulations with identifying numbers and *Federal Register* citations.

39. The rules in question are the Environmental Protection Agency's toxicity characteristics rule and its underground storage tank rule, the manufactured home construction and wind standards rule of the Department of Housing and Urban Development, and the Department of Health and Human Service's regulation prohibiting the sale of tobacco products to minors.

40. For three regulations we diverge slightly from the procedure explained in the text. For the Health and Human Services regulation on identification of potential organ donors, we estimated annual costs and benefits over only the five-year period for which the agency provided data, as we had no cost or benefit data in subsequent years. For the mammography rule issued by HHS, we took the agency's estimates of quality-adjusted life-years instead of estimating our own on the basis of their estimates of reductions in mortality risk. Finally, the Medicare rule on organ donors presented no information about the reductions in mortality risk. We therefore estimated the number of statistical lives saved from the

agency's estimates of life-years gained by assuming that the average number of life-years gained per death averted was seventeen. That figure was the lowest among comparable values in our database.

41. See Hahn (1996) for details.

42. Our latency assumptions are twenty-five years for lung cancer, ten years for other cancers, and two years for heart disease and stroke.

43. We make no other adjustments for countervailing risks because we have no information indicating that the agencies' analyses neglect such risks, although such neglect is important in some cases. See, for example, Lutter and Wolz (1997).

44. This estimate, which is consistent with the value of an additional year of life used by the Environmental Protection Agency in its reports to Congress on the benefits and costs of clean air, may be excessively high; see U.S. Environmental Protection Agency (1997; 1999a). The EPA's Science Advisory Board, in its final letter to the agency on the 1999 report, stated that it believed that values assigned to reductions in premature mortality from air pollution are "likely to be biased upwards" (U.S. Environmental Protection Agency 1999b, 2). In addition, the estimate is substantially greater than the estimate of roughly $100,000 per life-year suggested by Garber and Phelps (1997).

45. Expressing those unit costs in terms of cost per discounted statistical life-year rather than discounted statistical life does not significantly change the ranking of the rules in table 3-1 or the range of cost-effectiveness estimates. The ranking changes because rules regulating mammography standards and occupational exposure to methylene chloride are less attractive when evaluated in terms of costs per life-year gained. The FDA's mammography rule declines in rank because we use the agency's estimate of quality-adjusted life-years instead of calculating life-years, as we did for the other rules. OSHA's regulation limiting exposure to methylene chloride changed its rank because its benefits include avoided injuries as well as cancer cases avoided. The range in cost-effectiveness spans five orders of magnitude regardless of how public health improvements are measured.

46. That review is consistent with Goklany (1992), Morrall (1986), Hahn (1999), Tengs and Graham (1996), Viscusi (1996), and Lutter and Morrall (1994). Heinzerling (1998) criticized that approach for a variety of reasons, including the large uncertainty in the estimates of costs and benefits. While we readily admit that the calculations are subject to substantial uncertainty, strong evi-

dence exists that the effectiveness of lifesaving investments is likely to vary by at least a factor of 10,000. Thus, governments interested in investing in greater reductions in risk have ample opportunities to do so without expending additional resources.

47. For simplicity, we refer in this monograph to the Lutter, Morrall, and Viscusi (1999) cutoff as $15 million and, in a sensitivity analysis, $10 million and $50 million. Those values have been converted to 1995 dollars in our analysis ($17.3 million, $12 million, and $58 million, respectively). All other dollar values, in the text or figures, are in 1995 dollars.

48. See Viscusi (1994a).

49. See Tengs et al. (1995).

50. See Hahn (1999).

References

Central Intelligence Agency. 1998. *World Factbook 1998*. Washington, D.C.: Government Printing Office.

Chapman, Kenneth, and Govind Hariharan. 1994. "Controlling for Causality in the Link from Income to Mortality." *Journal of Risk and Uncertainty* 8: 85–93.

Cross, Frank. 1995. "When Environmental Regulations Kill: The Role of Health–Health Analysis." *Ecology Law Quarterly* 22: 729–82.

Duleep, Harriet. 1986. "Measuring the Effect of Income on Adult Mortality Using Longitudinal Administrative Record Data." *Journal of Human Resources* 20: 238–51.

Ettner, Susan L. 1996. "New Evidence on the Relationship between Income and Health." *Journal of Health Economics* 15: 67–86.

Garber, Alan, and Charles E. Phelps. 1997. "Economic Foundations of Cost-Effectiveness Analysis." *Journal of Health Economics* 16: 1–31.

Goklany, Indur. 1992. "Rationing Health Care While Writing Blank Checks for Environmental Hazards." *Regulation* (Summer 1992): 14–15.

Graham, John D., and Jonathan B. Wiener. 1995. *Risks vs. Risks: Tradeoffs in Protecting Health and the Environment*. Cambridge: Harvard University Press.

Hahn, Robert W. 1996. "Regulatory Reform: What Do the Government's Numbers Tell Us?" in *Risks, Costs, and Lives Saved: Getting Better Results from Regulation*, edited by Robert W. Hahn. New York and Washington, D.C.: Oxford University Press and AEI Press.

———. 1999. *Regulatory Reform: Assessing the Government's Numbers*. Working Paper 99-6. Washington, D.C.: AEI-Brookings Joint Center for Regulatory Studies.

Hahn, Robert W., Jason K. Burnett, Yee-Ho Chan, Elizabeth A. Mader, and Petrea R. Moyle. 2000. "Assessing the Quality of Regulatory

Impact Analyses." *Harvard Journal of Law and Public Policy* 23 (3): 859–85.

Harrison, David, Jr. 1975. *Who Pays for Clean Air: The Cost and Benefit Distribution of Automobile Emission Standards.* Cambridge: Ballinger.

Heinzerling, Lisa. 1998. "Regulatory Costs of Mythic Proportions." *Yale Law Journal* 107 (7): 1981.

Keeney, Ralph L. 1990. "Mortality Risks Induced by Economic Expenditures." *Risk Analysis* 10: 147–59.

———. 1994. "Mortality Risks Induced by the Costs of Regulations." *Journal of Risk and Uncertainty* 8: 95–110.

———. 1997. "Estimating Fatalities Induced by the Economic Costs of Regulations." *Journal of Risk and Uncertainty* 14 (1): 5–24.

Lamont, Douglas, Louise Parker, Martin White, Nigel Unwin, Stuart M. A. Bennett, Malanie Cohen, David Richardson, Heather O. Dickinson, Ashley Adamson, K. G. M. M. Alberti, and Alan W. Craft. 2000. "Risk of Cardiovascular Disease Measured by Carotid Intima-Media Thickness at Age 49–51: Lifecourse Study." *British Medical Journal* 320: 273–78.

Lave, Lester B. 1981. *The Strategy of Social Regulation: Decision Frameworks for Policy.* Washington, D.C.: Brookings Institution.

Lutter, Randall, and John F. Morrall III. 1994. "Health–Health Analysis: A New Way to Evaluate Health and Safety Regulation." *Journal of Risk and Uncertainty* 8: 43–66.

Lutter, Randall, and Christopher Wolz. 1997. "UV-B Screening by Tropospheric Ozone: Implications for the National Ambient Air Quality Standard." *Environmental Science and Technology* 31:142a–46a.

Lutter, Randall, John F. Morrall III, and W. Kip Viscusi. 1999. "The Cost-per-Life-Saved Cutoff for Safety-Enhancing Regulations." *Economic Inquiry* 37 (4): 599–608.

McGinnis, J. Michael, and William H. Foege. 1993. "Actual Causes of Death in the United States." *Journal of the American Medical Association* 270 (18): 2207–12.

Morrall, John F., III. 1986. "A Review of the Record." *Regulation* (November/December): 25–34.

Pritchett, Lant, and Lawrence Summers. 1996. "Wealthier Is Healthier." *Journal of Human Resources* 31 (4): 840–68.

Smith, James P. 1999. "Healthy Bodies, Thick Wallets: The Dual Relation between Health and Economic Status." *Journal of Economic Perspectives* 13 (2): 145–66.

Steger, Wilbur A. 1988. *Balancing the Risks and Benefits of Regulation for Health Purposes.* Pittsburgh: CONSAD Research Corporation.

Sunstein, Cass R. 1996. "Health–Health Tradeoffs." *University of Chicago Law Review* 63: 1533–73.

Tengs, Tammy O., and John D. Graham. 1996. "The Opportunity Costs of Haphazard Social Investments in Life-Saving." In *Risks, Costs, and Lives Saved: Getting Better Results from Regulation,* edited by Robert W. Hahn. New York and Washington, D.C.: Oxford University Press and AEI Press.

Tengs, Tammy O., Miriam E. Adams, Joseph S. Pliskin, Dana Gelb-Safran, Joanna E. Siegel, Michael C. Weinstein, and John D. Graham. 1995. "Five-Hundred Life-Saving Interventions and Their Cost-Effectiveness." *Risk Analysis* 15: 369–90.

Tietenberg, Thomas. 1996. *Environmental and Natural Resource Economics,* 4th ed. New York: HarperCollins.

U.S. Environmental Protection Agency. 1997. *The Benefits and Costs of the Clean Air Act: 1970 to 1990.* Washington, D.C.: Government Printing Office.

———. 1999a. *The Benefits and Costs of the Clean Air Act 1990 to 2010: EPA Report to Congress.* EPA-410-R-99-001. Washington, D.C.: Government Printing Office.

———. 1999b. *The Clean Air Act Amendments (CAAA) Section 812 Prospective Study of Costs and Benefits (1999): Advisory by the Advisory Council on Clean Air Compliance Analysis: Costs and Benefits of the CAAA.* October 29, 1999. EPA-SAB-Council-ADV-00-002. Washington, D.C.: Government Printing Office.

U.S. Food and Drug Administration. 1993. "Food Labeling Regulations." *Federal Register* 58: 2927.

U.S. Office of Management and Budget. 1999. *Report to Congress on the Benefits and Costs of Federal Regulations.* Washington, D.C.: Government Printing Office.

Viscusi, W. Kip. 1994a. "Mortality Effects of Regulatory Costs and Policy Evaluation Criteria." *RAND Journal of Economics* 25 (1): 94–109.

———. 1996. "The Dangers of Unbounded Commitments to Regulate Risk." In *Risks, Costs, and Lives Saved: Getting Better Results from Regulation,* edited by Robert W. Hahn. New York and Washington, D.C.: Oxford University Press and AEI Press.

———, ed. 1994b. The Mortality Costs of Regulatory Expenditures, A Special Issue of the Journal of Risk and Uncertainty. *Journal of Risk and Uncertainty* 8 (4).

Viscusi, W. Kip, and Richard J. Zeckhauser. 1994. "The Fatality and Injury Costs of Expenditures." *Journal of Risk and Uncertainty* 8 (4): 19–41.

Walls, Margaret, and Jean Hanson. 1999. "Distributional Aspects of an Environmental Tax Shift: The Case of Motor Vehicle Emissions Taxes." *National Tax Journal* 52 (1): 53–65.

Warren, Edward W., and Gary E. Marchant. 1993. "'More Good Than Harm': A First Principle for Environmental Agencies and Reviewing Courts." *Ecology Law Quarterly* 20: 379–439.

Wiener, Jonathan B. 1998. "Managing the Iatrogenic Risks of Risk Management." *Risk: Health, Safety, and Environment* 9: 39–82.

Wildavsky, Aaron. 1980. "Richer Is Safer." *Public Interest* 60: 23–29.

Wolfson, Michael, Geoff Rowe, Jane Gentleman, and Monica Tomiak. 1992. *Career Earnings and Death: A Longitudinal Analysis of Older Canadian Men.* Research Paper Series No. 45. Ottawa, Canada: Statistics Canada.

About the Authors

Robert W. Hahn is director of the AEI-Brookings Joint Center for Regulatory Studies, a resident scholar at the American Enterprise Institute, and a research associate at Harvard University.

Randall W. Lutter is a fellow at the AEI-Brookings Joint Center for Regulatory Studies and a resident scholar at the American Enterprise Institute.

W. Kip Viscusi is the John F. Cogan, Jr., Professor of Law and Economics and director of the Program on Empirical Legal Studies at Harvard Law School.

J O I N T   C E N T E R

AEI-BROOKINGS JOINT CENTER FOR REGULATORY STUDIES

Director
Robert W. Hahn

Codirector
Robert E. Litan

Fellows
Robert W. Crandall
Christopher C. DeMuth
Randall W. Lutter
Clifford M. Winston

In response to growing concerns about the impact of regulation on consumers, business, and government, the American Enterprise Institute and the Brookings Institution established the AEI-Brookings Joint Center for Regulatory Studies. The primary purpose of the center is to hold lawmakers and regulators more accountable by providing thoughtful, objective analysis of existing regulatory programs and new regulatory proposals. The Joint Center builds on AEI's and Brookings's impressive body of work over the past three decades that evaluated the economic impact of regulation and offered constructive suggestions for implementing reforms to enhance productivity and consumer welfare. The views in Joint Center publications are those of the authors and do not necessarily reflect the views of the staff, council of academic advisers, or fellows.

COUNCIL OF ACADEMIC ADVISERS